THE BLIGHTED

LIFE OF METHUSELAH.

BY

H. ROGER WILLIAMS, M. D.,

NASHVILLE, TENN.:
NATIONAL BAPTIST PUBLISHING BOARD,
1908

THE BLIGHTED LIFE OF METHUSELAH.

A TREATISE

FROM

GENESIS V:27.

SHOWING THE MANY OPPORTUNITIES WHICH METHUSELAH
HAD FOR MAKING A CHRISTIAN RECORD, AND HOW
BY LETTING THEM PASS UNNOTICED FOR
NINE HUNDRED AND SIXTY-NINE
YEARS, HE DIED AND
WAS LOST.

THE TREATISE

IS TO

SAINTS AND SINNERS

AS A WARNING AGAINST NEGLECTING
THE OPPORTUNITIES THAT COME TO THEM DAILY
FOR DOING SOMETHING TO MAKE THE WORLD BETTER FOR
THEIR HAVING LIVED IN IT, AND CLEAR THEIR
OWN PATHWAY TO ETERNAL GLORY.

BY

H. ROGER WILLIAMS, M. D.,

MOBILE, ALA.

H. ROGER WILLIAMS.

PREFACE.

With earnest hope that this little book may lead some sinner to repent, or arouse some slothful Christian from the spiritual stupor into which so many have fallen, I send it forth to all who care to peruse its pages.

What will become of it on the great ocean of opinions, whose thought waves, swept in billowy masses by the winds of controversy, lash the shores of Publication, and threaten to submerge this generation in a deluge of paper and printer's ink, I know not; but I am satisfied that "God, who has watched while my weary toils lasted, will give me a harvest for what I have done. In His name I send it forth."

THE AUTHOR.

CONTENTS.

8 *Contents.*

THE

BLIGHTED LIFE OF METHUSELAH.

CHAPTER I.

INTRODUCTORY.

The words which we use as a basis of argument are recorded in the twenty-seventh verse of
the fifth chapter of Genesis, and read thus: "And
all the days of Methuselah were nine hundred and
sixty-nine years; and he died." Statements of
a similar nature were made in referring to many
others of the antedeluvian patriarchs; but in this
particular case it ends the life history of a man
who had lived longer upon the earth than any
mortal of whom we have a record. Adam, Seth,
Enos, Cainan, Jared and Noah, all lived over nine
hundred years; (Gen. i:5-29) but Methuselah
outstripped them all in the race for longevity;
and, having reached his nine hundred and sixty-
ninth anniversary, like an exhausted ocean wave
struggling across the sea, he fell lifeless on the
shore of Time, and the Scriptures say "He died."

Now, it must be accepted as an axiom by every follower of Christ that the Scriptures are the revealed word of God, the various assumptions of eminent scholars to the contrary notwithstanding. Every word, every expression, every declaration made in the dear old Book is pregnant with truths, many of which, like the hidden treasures in the mountains of earth, are discovered after having been passed unnoticed for centuries.

"Search the Scriptures," is the advice of the Saviour to those who would make their way from the city of Destruction to the kingdom of God. (John v:39.)   All Scripture is by inspiration of God, and is profitable for doctrine, for reproof, for correction, for instruction in righteousness: that the man of God may be perfect, thoroughly furnished unto all good works."—2 Tim. iii:16, 17.

Almost every historic person in the Bible bears an appropriate name, not alone to designate him from other individuals, but the name was descriptive of the character and life of its possessor.

"Out of the ground the Lord God formed every beast of the field, and every fowl of the air; and brought them unto Adam to see what he would call them: and whatsoever Adam called every living creature, that was the name thereof." (Gen.

ii:19.) "And Abraham called the name of his son
that was born unto him, whom Sarah bare to him,
Isaac." (Gen. xxi:3.) "And Rachel said with
great wrestlings have I wrestled with my sister,
and I have prevailed: and she called his name
Naphtali." (Gen. xxx:8.) "And Joseph called the
name of the first born Manasseh: for God, said
he, hath made me forget all my toil, and all my
father's house." (Gen. xli:51.) Zipperah, the
Negro wife of Moses, for despising whom Miriam
was smitten with leprosy, and the marching army
of Israelites was forced to halt for seven days
(Numbers xii:15), gave birth to a son, and Moses
named him Gershom, for he said, "I have been a
stranger in a strange land" (Ex. ii:22); and when
the angel had made an explanation to Joseph of
what had happened to his virgin wife, he said,
(Matt. v:21), "She shall bring forth a son, and
thou shalt call his name Jesus; for he shall save
his people from their sins" (23 verse). "They
shall call his name Emmanuel, which being inter-
preted is, God with us."

The name of our hero is "Methuselah." It is
from two Hebrew words, "Methu," which means
"He dieth," and "Shalah," which means "He send-
eth out." Now, the problem that confronts us
is to know whether he died and was sent out of

the world to be preserved from some approaching calamity, or whether he died and was sent out from the presence of God. Either might be inferred from his name, and the effort of our research will be to gather the rays of Scripture truths, and, focusing them through the lens of Reason, by the electrical force of the Holy Spirit, produce a violet X-ray of logical conclusion, that we may know for a certainty whether Methuselah died and was sent out to enter the Paradise promised to the thief on the cross, or whether he died and was sent out to awake with Dives in the flames of eternal burning, where it is said, "There shall be weeping and gnashing of teeth." Imploring the Holy Spirit to aid us in the attempt to render transparent these hitherto opaque walls, and trusting God for the results, we turn to the discussion of our subject: The Blighted Life of Methuselah.

CHAPTER II.

THE LONG LIFE OF METHUSELAH.

Methuselah lived nine hundred and sixty-nine years, and, though many arguments have been produced to show that a year then was not the same as a year of to-day, the truth remains that Moses, the writer of the statement, was the founder of the Jewish religion, and nowhere in history can it be found that a year of to-day is less or more than the years spoken of elsewhere in the Bible. Numerous passages of Scripture tell us of years in such terms that there can be no shadow of doubt as to their length. Corn crops grow only once in our years of to-day. The forty-first chapter of Genesis tells of Pharaoh's dream concerning the seven years of plenty and the seven years of famine. It tells of the gathering of crops and enlarging of barns in such explicit language that every one who reads it may know that the corn crops grew annually, just as they do to-day. In Genesis, Moses gives the life of Sarai, saying she was old and stricken in age, and had reached the

climacteric period of her life. Her husband was
ninety years old, and the statement that she had
passed the custom of women is evidence that
the years accounted to her were about the same
that we count to-day.

God inspired Moses to write the Book of Genesis, but the facts recorded are stated by Moses
in language with which he was thoroughly conversant. He was educated in all the wisdom and
science of Egypt, and he was familiar with the
signs of the zodiac and their markings of years.
I believe there was no shadow of doubt in his
mind as to the truth of his statement when he
wrote the words, "And all the days of Methuselah were nine hundred and sixty-nine years, and
he died." And because I find everything in the
Bible which I can comprehend is true, I believe
with my whole heart that the rest is true also,
and only regret that my understanding is so
blurred, and my knowledge is so limited, that I
cannot comprehend the depth of what I believe,
but cannot explain.

Methuselah lived nine hundred and sixty-nine
years, and if, in the length of our short life, men
born in ignorance, can grow to manhood, get an
education, change the very face of the earth, and
startle the universe by their wonderful achieve-

ments, what must have been the opportunities afforded Methuselah for development along all lines while living through nine hundred and sixty-nine years? The ghost of premature death had never been seen, for all who lived before him, neared or passed the ninth century mile-post in the path of human existence, except his father, Enoch, who, walking with God, grew tired of mortality in his three hundred and sixty-fifth year, and went to the Great Beyond.

The days of our life are three score years and ten; his nearly a thousand. You will have some idea of the vast period of time which his long life covered when I tell you if he had been born in the days of Peter the Hermit, A.D. 1050, he would have been a man twenty-seven years old when Jerusalem, which for a long time had been in the hands of the Calif of Omar, passed under the Turkman domination. He would have been forty-nine years old when Peter the Hermit aroused the fiery piety and chivalry of Europe and led to that extraordinary succession of holy wars, which restored the tomb of our Lord and the Holy City back into Christian hands. He would have been four hundred and forty-two years old when Columbus discovered America; he would have seen all the advancements of civilization since the

Mayflower landed at Plymouth. He would have been eight hundred and sixty-three years old when Abraham Lincoln signed the proclamation which unbound the fetters from four and a half million souls and banished slavery from the United States. He could have fought in the Spanish-American war; taken part in all the political harangues of to-day, and still have one hundred and forty-two years to prepare for death, which would not be due to come to him until every person now alive would be dead, and the calendars of the world were showing the eclipses and moon changes for the year two thousand and forty-nine. From his knowledge of the past, Methuselah could inaugurate movements which it would take him centuries to accomplish without ever being harassed by the fear that death would interrupt his plans.

If, within the short space of time that men live to-day, they can develop every faculty of the soul so that the understanding can compass the earth, measure the heavenly bodies and foreknow each eclipse to a minute many years before it comes to pass; yea, if within the short limit of three score years and ten, our intellect can grasp the torchlight of science, and, entering the halls of nature, unlock the secret chambers of creative skill and harnessing the fiery elements send them on errands as swift-winged messengers; if men born within this century have threaded the world with railroads, taught inanimate machinery to speak with human distinctness, and communicate with those in distant parts through the medium of wireless telegraphy; what must have been the opportunities afforded Methuselah while living through nine hundred and sixty-nine years!

Did he seize those opportunities as an eagle would its fleeing prey, or did he allow them to pass unnoticed as would swine rare gems and valuable diamonds, not knowing of nor caring for their intrinsic value? Must we declare that he is happy with the blest simply because no brother's blood cried from the ground against him as it did against Cain? Shall we call him a righteous father simply because he is not referred to as taking an active part in the sins of his day? No, dear reader, God's plan has never changed with reference to the salvation of this world.

CHAPTER III.

THE CREATION OF THE WORLD.

Out in the fathomless ocean of immensity, God placed the sun-dial of Love. He set it with the energy of Omnipotence, and the shadow of time began to move off in waves of action toward the shores of eternity. Upon one of those waves God launched a creation called heaven and earth, weird and without form; "And the Spirit of God moved upon the face of the waters" (Gen. i:2), amid the awful darkness of that mighty deep. God spoke, and His words caused the heaven to oscillate with tremendous ponderosity; the vibrations from which moved off through the luminous ether in such rapid succession and at such a terrific rate of speed they illuminated the universe when God said, "Let there be light."

At the simple command of God, the firmament leaped forth from the womb of Time, and stationed itself as a sentinel to separate the waters above from those below. With the great dipper of authority, God lifted all the waters under the heavens, poured them into the hollow places called seas, and let the dry land appear. He breathed on the earth, and the soil became pregnant and gave birth to all manner of vegetation, the blossoming flowers from which perfumed the air with a sweet aroma. He touched the water of the sea, and it conceived and bore an abundance of moving creatures; some rising above the waters and flying through the heavens, while others, called fish, went swimming through the deep. He spoke to the earth, and the dust became vivified and, assuming various shapes, began to move about in the form of all the different creatures that fill the earth with animation. Some of the creatures, though perfectly formed and given a full set of faculties, are so small and yet so numerous that eight hundred million worlds like ours would be required to maintain a human population equal to the number of these tiny creatures that live and move in a cubic inch of space. All the myriads and myriads of worlds that sweep through space—massive creations in themselves— many of them immensely larger than our own, running wider revolutions, and drawing after them brighter trains; these, and myriads more of worlds that do not come within the borders of our solar family, were all formed from an atom of nothing by the fiat of Almighty God, and, through all, there is evidence of a divine plan and arrangement. Man was the crowning triumph of creative effort. He is greater than the world in which he lives, and there is more mystery in the union of the soul and the body than there is in the creation of all the systems of worlds that make up the universe. His anatomy, his physical formation, his intellectual and spiritual nature, together with the fact that he was given the power of speech and the ability to balance himself and walk erect, give man a pre-eminence over all the other objects of God's creation. He was the last, as well as the fairest, of God's divine works, and was not brought into existence until everything for his comfort had been made, and all preparations for his reception and happiness were complete. The earth had been fashioned in all its transcendant beauty, and Eden had been enriched with all her stores of verdant foliage. Then, while surrounded by all the created hosts and the efflorescence of nature, amid anthems of joy and jubilations of praise from beasts and birds and flowers and fish and all the millions of created forms that joined in the universal chorus, "when the morning stars sang together and all the Sons of God shouted for joy," God, as a crowning cap-sheaf to his handiwork, said, "Let us make man in our image, after our likeness."

Why did not God speak man into existence, as he did everything else? Why was it necessary for the mighty God, the everlasting Father, the wonderful Creator, to call a consultation before making man? Why did He not rend the rocks asunder with the thunder of His awful voice, and, calling, as did Christ at the grave of Lazarus, bid man come forth from the bowels of the earth? The only reasonable answer is this: Man was the earthly reflection of the heavenly glory of God, and, as such, all heaven was asked to assist in making him, that he might be within himself a perfect reflection of all that heaven was. "So God created man in His own image;" "and breathed into his nostrils the breath of life; and man became a living soul," possessing all the attributes and graces of Deity, and endowed with immortality of existence.

CHAPTER IV.

THE DIVINE PURPOSE OF CREATION.

Remember, dear reader, this was not absolutely necessary, for God is omniscient, as well as omnipotent. He could have made man perfect without the aid or assistance of any of the heavenly host. But it was in the divine purpose of God to have all heaven interested in man, and so all heaven was consulted before he was created. And so also it is in the divine purpose of God to have man interested in the salvation of man, and no man can have hope of an eternal abode in the kingdom of Christ, unless he is in perfect accord with heaven's chief aim—the restoration of man back into the image of God.

When man transgressed the law of God and fell from his high and holy estate, his graces and virtues, like the good things of Prometheus, when Pandora opened the box of the Greek's first man, took wings and flew away. All that was left to Adam was hope, and penitently kneel-

(22)

ing upon it, he prayed to God for forgiveness. God, who looked down in tender compassion on the prostrate form of fallen man, as he wept and mourned over his lost estate, graciously pardoned him, and consoled him with the promise that "His seed should bruise the serpent's head." Though man had lost his physical immortality, his soul would live forever; though he could no longer inhabit the blissful shades of an earthly Eden, he could become an expectant of the kingdom of God. He could no longer come into existence full grown and full of wisdom. The faculties are all there, but they must be developed. Man comes into existence innocent, but ignorant. He is physiologically perfect, but he is utterly helpless. He is capable of infinite wisdom and goodness, but he must be instructed. He is his own free moral agent, and must choose for himself his eternal abode. The devil and all the hosts of hell beset him as soon as he is born, and try by all the subtlety of his satanic strategy to attract him hellward. The sweet influence of the Holy Spirit seeks, through the word of truth, to restore him back into the image of his God. It is the divine purpose of God that man assist in this great work. He is eminently fitted for it, and he saves his own soul only by seeking the salvation of others.

CHAPTER V.

A Vision of Adam.

In a vision I can see Adam, the father of the human race and transgressor of heaven's law. He has been hurled from the throne of power, and driven from the garden made for him by his Creator. His kingdom has been confiscated. His lordship and power of authority have become things of the past. The beasts and birds no longer obey his mandates, but make the woods ring with hideous sounds, as they prey upon each other. The soft zephyrs which gently disturbed the sweet-smelling foliage of Eden, having become vexed and lashed themselves into wrathsome fury, are sweeping through the land in death-dealing tornadoes and cyclones. His children, nourished from the breast of the same mother, have quarreled, and Cain having slain his brother and buried him in the soil, has fled as a fugitive from justice, almost breaking the heart of his mother, who weeps and mourns because her sons are no longer where she can fondle them in her

(24)

loving embrace. The angels of Peace and Happiness, sent from the courts of glory to abide with man, have spread their wings and taken their flight from the sin-cursed earth. Discord can be heard in every hand, and over the whole realm of nature the evil genius of sin is now presiding.

Year after year, decade after decade, century after century passes, increasing the number of Adam's posterity, and augmenting his grief and sorrow. I can see him, with a deep-wrinkled, care-worn face, down the cheeks of which tears of remorse are streaming. Decrepitude has visited him and made an exchange of age for youth. Feeble and old, he leans for support on the promise of God. Around him are gathered a company of his posterity, the older of whom look thoughtfully upon the ground, while the younger ones look · anxiously about, as if fearful of some approaching danger. As I watch the company, I behold Adam sighing as if his heart would break, as tenderly he beckons to Eve, who with feeble step and bended form, leaning upon the broad shoulders of Seth for support, cautiously wends her way to him and takes a seat by his side. Her face shows signs of much bodily suffering, and her hair is white with age, but the tender look of a mother's love can still be seen in her sunken eyes as she scans the group surrounding her, as if to see that none are absent. The sun is gradually sinking behind the western hills, the refracted rays from which stream off among the trees, giving a golden tinge to the verdant foliage. Every hillside, valley and plain, as far as the eye can behold, is a scene of such indescribable beauty we are forced to exclaim with the Psalmist, "The heavens declare the glory of God: and the firmament showeth his handiwork." (Psa. xix:1.)

As the last rays of the setting sun fade into twilight, Adam rises to his feet and addresses the company in a low, tremulous voice. He recites a passage from the book of his experience. He tells them how he sinned against the law of God, and the consequent effects it had upon him. He tells them, as he had heard it from the lips of God, about the war in heaven; the overthrow of Satan and his cohorts; the creation of the world; his stay in the Garden of Eden; the allurements of the evil one; how he seeks to apostatize the human race and alienate it from God. He tells them of how the Lord God made coats of skin and clothed them, of His promise to redeem them from the curse of the broken law, and admonishes them to serve the Lord with sacrifice, and believe with all their heart that He will keep His promise. He contrasts his present sorrow with his long-lost happiness, and as the pent-up sorrow of his soul overwhelms him, hot "Tears of penitential grief burst forth from every eye."

Eve lifts her voice, which has not yet lost its Eden sweetness, and leads the evening hymn, the words of which I cannot understand, by reason of the sobbing emotions of Adam, augmented by the wails of the weeping company. Adam lifts his hands toward the heavens, and in humiliation, every member of the company falls prostrate in the dust to pour out the agony of their soul in prayer to God. Prayer is over, and all retire for the night, satisfied that God will watch over them while they sleep, and protect them from every harm.

Now, remember, dear reader, the Bible does not say that Adam was ever visited by any of his posterity; neither does it aver that he was a preacher of righteousness; but the thoughtful reader of God's Word will bear witness that I have not overdrawn the picture.

CHAPTER VI.

EVIDENCE THAT ADAM TAUGHT HIS POSTERITY.

In the fourth chapter of the Book of Genesis, the second verse, we are told that Cain was a farmer; Abel, a shepherd. The second, third and fourth verses of the same chapter tell us that Cain offered fruit; Abel, a choice lamb. The fourth and fifth verses aver that God had respect for the offering of Abel, but rejected the offering of Cain. The eighth verse says Cain rose up against his brother and slew him; and the seventeenth verse tells how Cain, after murdering his brother, wandered off in the Land of Nod, raised a family and built a city. Now, all these actions were the result of knowledge previously obtained; for it is an axiom in philosophy that no finite mind can conceive an entirely new thing. But, whence came they in possession of such knowledge as would enable them to know what would be the results of their efforts? Where had they ever heard a musical instrument? How did they know that it were possible to take life from a living organism by administering a blow upon the same? Who taught

(28)

Jabal to dwell in tents and herd cattle? (Gen. iv:20). And where did Tubal Cain conceive the idea that brass and iron could be moulded into different forms and polished to a luster? You cannot say they happened to imbibe the ideas which led to those various pursuits by chance or force of circumstances. God held Cain accountable for not bringing as a sin offering the right kind of a sacrifice; and pronounced a curse upon him for murdering his brother, whose sacrifice was pleasing to the Lord. This is conclusive evidence that they had been instructed along those very lines, and there was no excuse to offer. God never holds any man responsible for a transgression until he has been instructed concerning its awful consequences. Paul says (Rom. vii:7-8), "I had not known sin, but by the law: for without the law sin is dead." Romans, fifth chapter, thirteenth verse, reads thus: "For until the law sin was in the world: but sin is not imputed where there is no law." And Jesus said (John xv:22), "If I had not come and spoken unto them, they had not had sin; but now they have no cloak for their sin." From this we conclude that these men had been instructed, and knew the results of their actions, and the kind of sacrifice that would be pleasing to their God.

But who taught them these things, and whence came they in possession of knowledge concerning things of which they had not dreamed? The only reasonable conclusion is to suppose that they were taught by the father of the human race, who, having spent many evenings conversing with his Maker, amid the shady boughs and sweet-smelling foliage of Eden, had been taught of God concerning everything pertaining to the interests of humanity. Knowing, as we do, the delight it is to children to visit their ancestors, and the relish with which aged parents tell their children of the wonderful exploits, daring deeds, hair-breadth escapes and awe-inspiring scenes which they have witnessed from time to time, we are sure that Adam was often surrounded by eager listeners, to whom he would give glowing accounts of the joy and sorrow, pleasure and pain, blessings and curses, plenty and poverty that had checkered his life from his creation. Through conversations like these, Adam, no doubt, told them how the transcendant beauty of this world was created by the omnipotence of Jehovah, giving them a minute description of the Garden of Eden, and repeating to them, as he had heard from the lips of his Creator, how the orchestra of heaven played the sweet symphonies of Paradise; and the angel choir led in the chorus, "and the morning stars sang together, and all the sons of God shouted for joy" when the world was created.   (Job xxxviii: 7).   He reiterated to them the story of the fall, of the promise to redeem them (Gen. iii:15), of how the Lord God made coats of skin (Gen. ii: 21), and clothed them; of how he was driven from the garden to till the ground (Gen. iii:23) from whence he was taken, and how God placed angels with ever-turning, flaming swords at the gates of Eden (Gen. iii:24) to keep the way of the tree of life.   Many of these scenes, no doubt, were described by Adam in such graphic word-paintings that they became as real pictures to his eager listeners.

Thus Cain got his idea of farming, Abel of sheep-raising, and what would be a pleasing sacrifice.   Through these talks, no doubt, Adam taught his posterity how to gain a livelihood, and thus began the branching out into different pursuits, according as different ones were impressed differently from listening to his conversations; while those of an inventive turn of mind were led to attempt a reproduction of some of the things which Adam described as having seen and heard. Thus began the imitative efforts which resulted in the invention of the loom for cloth weaving, the working in brass and iron, and the invention of musical instruments. But these inventors and craftsmen were descendants of Cain (Gen. iv: 20-22), who wandered away from Adam to the other side of the Garden of Eden (Gen. iv:16), and built a beautiful city in the Land of Nod.

CHAPTER VII.

The Difference Between Saints and Sinners.

Adam was deeply interested in the salvation of men, and the characteristic difference between the heaven-bound mortals and those destined to eternal banishment from the presence of God is a longing interest in the saving of souls and teaching men what God would have them know. Every man, from Adam on down to the present day, is offered an opportunity to help in the work of trying to redeem man from the curse of the broken law. Adam, as we have shown, was a preacher of righteousness, Seth was called "the appointed," and Moses tells us that Enoch and Noah walked with God. The plan of salvation is such that man saves his own soul only by saving others. Every man is expected to help, and Christ, the Captain of our salvation, declares, "He that is not with me is against me; and he that gathereth not with me scattereth." (Matt. xii:30.) The man or woman who sits idly by and allows a soul to be lost without using every available effort in the attempt to

(33)

save that soul will be required to give an account for the same at the bar of God.

Joe Stoker, the brakeman, was ordered to hasten to the curve and wave his lantern that the coming express train might know that there was danger ahead. He delayed, leisurely pulling on his overcoat, then getting a drink of whiskey, then lighting his pipe. When he heard the whistle of the engine coming around the curve, he hastened with all possible speed to obey the command he had received, but, alas, too late. The fast train came bursting around the curve, telescoping the wrecked train, and hurling its cargo of human souls into eternity. When Joe Stoker was found the next morning, his mind was gone, and, a wild maniac, he stood in a barn swinging his empty lantern before an imaginary train and crying in the agony of his soul, "Oh, that I had! Oh, that I had!" With the world full of work that needs to be done; with human nature so constituted that often a pleasant word or a trifling assistance may stem the tide of disaster for some fellowman, or clear his path to heaven; with our own faculties so arranged that in honest, earnest, persistent endeavor we find our highest good, and with countless noble examples to encourage us to dare and do, each moment brings us to the threshold of some new opportunity for improving the stock of the human race. For God's sake, do not let them pass lest when it is too late, like Joe Stoker, you will be heard to say, "Oh, that I had! Oh, that I had!"

CHAPTER VIII.

METHUSELAH CONTEMPORARY WITH ADAM.

According to the dates given in the fifth chapter of Genesis, Adam was one hundred and thirty years old when he begat Seth; Seth was one hundred and five years old when he begat Enos; Enos was ninety years old when he begat Cainan; Cainan was seventy years old when he begat Mahalaleel; Mahalaleel was sixty-five years old when he begat Jared; Jared was one hundred and sixty-two years old when he begat Enoch; Enoch was sixty-five years old when he begat Methuselah. Now, if Adam was created in the year one, reckoning from the beginning, then, we find, by comparing the dates above given, that Seth was born in the year one hundred and thirty; Enos, in the year two hundred and thirty-five; Cainan, in the year three hundred and twenty-five; Mahalaleel, in the year three hundred and ninety-five; Jared, in the year four hundred and sixty; Enoch, in the year six hundred and twenty-two; and Methuselah, in the year six hundred and eighty-seven.

(36)

Now, the records show that Adam lived nine hundred and thirty years; and if he were six hundred and eighty-seven years old when Methuselah was born, then it follows that Methuselah was two hundred and forty-three years old when Adam died.

When Frederick, the Emperor of Saxony, was told by a celebrated genealogist, that a copy of his pedigree was preserved in the ark of Noah, he neglected all the affairs of state, and wandered about from place to place in a vain attempt to find Noah's ark. And how can we for a moment believe that any man could live on earth two hundred and forty-three years and not seek the acquaintance and companionship of Adam, the only human being that was ever permitted to talk with God face to face (Gen. iii:8) ?

By comparing the descendants of Adam through Seth with those who were descendants from Cain, we find that Jabal, Jubal and Tubal-Cain—the last three sons mentioned in the lineage of Cain —were all three of the same generation, and contemporary with Methuselah, who, as we have shown, was born two hundred and forty-three years before Adam died. That Jabal, Jubal and Tubal-Cain were frequent visitors of Adam there can be no doubt, for they became the world's first inventors and craftsmen, as we have previously shown, and Adam was the only source from which they could have gained the knowledge necessary to prepare them for such mighty works. But Jabal, Jubal and Tubal-Cain were descendants of Cain, who dwelt in the Land of Nod, on the other side of the Garden of Eden. And if those who lived in another part of the then-known world had knowledge of Adam and visited him often enough to grasp ideas that developed into wonderful inventions for the advancement of civilization, then I am certain, beyond a shadow of doubt, that Methuselah, descending from Seth, the appointed (Gen. iv:25), through Enoch who walked with God (Gen. v:24), and living upon the earth for two hundred and forty-three years before Adam left it, was thoroughly acquainted with the father of the human race, and knew of sin and its awful effects upon the soul. Works of righteousness were as needful then as now, and any failure on his part to serve the Lord was as noticeable then as it would be now. The law of God has always been the same. He himself says (Mal. iii:4-6), "I am the Lord, I change not."

CHAPTER IX.

Having shown that Methuselah was acquainted
with Adam and knew his career, let us now pro-
ceed to study his life history and see who else
he may have known among the antedeluvian patriarchs while living through nine hundred and
sixty-nine years. When he was one hundred and
eighty-seven years old, he begat Lamech; and
when Lamech was one hundred and eighty-two
years old, he begat Noah. Thus Methuselah was
three hundred and sixty-nine years old when Noah
was born.

Adam, having been created in the year one,
and living nine hundred and thirty years, died in
the year nine hundred and thirty. Seth was born
in the year one hundred and thirty, and living
nine hundred and twelve years, died in the year
ten hundred and forty. Enos was born in the
year two hundred and thirty-five, and, living nine
hundred and five years, died in the year eleven

(39)

hundred and forty. Cainan was born in the year three hundred and twenty-five, and, living nine hundred and ten years, died in the year twelve hundred and thirty-five. Mahalaleel was born in the year three hundred and ninety-five, and, living eight hundred and ninety-five years, died in the year twelve hundred and ninety. Jared was born in the year four hundred and sixty, and, living nine hundred and sixty-two years, died in the year fourteen hundred and twenty-two. Enoch was born in the year six hundred and twenty-two, and, being taken by the Lord, with whom he walked three hundred years after his son was born, he left the world in the year nine hundred and eighty-seven. Methuselah was born in the year six hundred and eighty-seven, and, living nine hundred and sixty-nine years, died in the year sixteen hundred and fifty-six. Lamech was born in the year eight hundred and seventy-four, and, living seven hundred and seventy-seven years, he died in the year sixteen hundred and fifty-one. Noah was born in the year ten hundred and fifty-six, and, living nine hundred and fifty years, died in the year two thousand and six.

From the above facts, it is clearly apparent to all that Methuselah was contemporary with all who lived from the time Adam was six hundred and eighty-seven years old down to the time when his grandson, Noah, was a man of six hundred summers. He saw the death, and, no doubt, attended the funeral of Adam, Seth, Enos, Cainan, Mahalaleel, Jared, and his own son, Lamech, who, living seven hundred and seventy-seven years, died five years before his father, Methuselah.

Now, if for argument's sake, we should grant that it were possible for Methuselah to have lived for two hundred and eighty-seven years near Adam, and yet not know him, is it not reasonable to suppose that, being contemporary with all who lived before the flood, he knew why he was forced to earn a living by the sweat of his brow? Am I not justified in the sight of heaven when I say he was thoroughly conversant with God's law, and was in possession of the knowledge which the world had at that time? Yes, dear reader, I am satisfied that I only speak that which is the decision of every thinking mind who reads these pages, and to which, I believe, the angels of glory, if called upon to bear witness, would say, "Amen."

CHAPTER X.

Methuselah's Opportunities for Instructing Others.

Age naturally awakens our respect, and Methuselah must have been much revered by reason of the longevity which he enjoyed. He could speak as an eye-witness of the world's happenings from Adam to his grandson Noah. Slowly the centuries had unfolded one by one before him, as leisurely he walked along from his cradle to the grave. Cedars which he planted in his youth had grown old and rotted down. Firm rocks on the mountain, down whose sides the waters flowed, had been washed away, while he, unharmed by the grim monster Death, was allowed to live on amid the ever-verdant vales of waving palm trees and sweet-smelling foliage of vine-clad hills.

He was infinitely better prepared to be a preacher of righteousness than any man that ever lived, for from observation he had seen the results of sinning against God, and the advantage his father had above the world by walking with him. He could reason from cause to effect, and conversely,

(42)

concerning many things, which to others of those living were complicated problems.

He could have given to the world proverbs of far more import and meaning than ever fell from the lips of Solomon; for Solomon's life was not longer than a life of to-day; and though he, as an unrestrained polygamist, indulged the unsatiable lust of the flesh until a thousand women were calling him husband, Methuselah could tell of experiences that would pale into insignificance the most voluptuous scenes of Solomon's gilded palace. Methuselah had seen women whose beauty was beyond the power of words to describe, and who, in sensual lust and alluring carnality, were such temptations that the legates of glory —the sons of God—could not withstand their amorous alkahests (Gen., vi:2-4) and married them, producing a peculiarly large-bodied posterity called giants. Solomon could only say (Prov. i:8), "My son, hear the instruction of thy father." Methuselah lived until his great-grandsons were a hundred years old; and he must have been often consulted for counsel and advice, for he was one hundred and eighty-seven years older than any other man upon the earth.

CHAPTER XI.

METHUSELAH'S OPPORTUNITIES FOR FAVOR WITH GOD.

Methuselah's life, as we have said, was a long one. The dark cloud of immorality, which was no bigger than the palm of the hand when he came into existence, had spread over the entire heavens of moral purity from pole to pole, shutting off the refracted rays from the "Son of righteousness." Man had become so depraved that "every imagination of the thoughts of his heart was only evil continually." (Gen. vi:6.) The sons of God, through the daughters of men, had filled the land with giants. They were a warlike people, and became valiant for their strength and courage. Sin and immorality filled the atmosphere with such a foul stench that the odor was diffused through the rarefied ether of the celestial world, and reached the nostrils of the King of Kings. The thunder of His awful word reverberated from the hills of Zion as the wrath of God was kindled, and He exclaimed: "I will destroy man whom I have created from the face of the earth; both

(44)

man, and beast, and the creeping thing, and the
fowls of the air; for it repenteth me that I have
made them." (Gen. vi:7.)

Surely a man occupying the strategic point in
the affairs of men that Methuselah held could not
have escaped the all-seeing eye of God, or the sacred historians if he did anything worthy of the
notice of God or man. He was the son of Enoch,
a man who, by the firmness of his desire to grow
better, was able, by daily effort (notwithstanding
the sin and immorality which surrounded him on
every hand) to bring under subjection every evil
desire and walk with God for three hundred years.
He was the grandfather of Noah, who, Peter tells
us, "was a preacher of righteousness;" and the author of Genesis described as "walking with God."
Doubtless, he was thoroughly acquainted with Lamech of Cain; had held many conversations with
him, and heard him when he exclaimed, "I have
slain a man to my wounding, and a young man
to my hurt." (Gen. iv:23.)

Numerous incidents connected with the time in
which he lived prove that the actions of God toward men in the days of Methuselah were exactly
the same as they are to-day, and His law, though,
perhaps, unwritten, was diligently taught, and
thoroughly understood, and, therefore, was as

binding upon the human heart as it is to-day. When Adam, who by his disobedience, had brought death to the entire world, showed signs of repentance for his sin committed, God heard his penitent cry, forgave him his transgression, and consoled him with a promise that his seed should bruise the serpent's head. When Abel brought of the firstling of his flock and offered it as an oblation for his sins, "God had respect unto Abel and to his offering." (Gen. iv:4.) When Cain failed to bring the right kind of a sacrifice, it was rejected. When he had slain his brother and wept over the justly deserved curse which God pronounced upon him, mercy was shown him, and God set a mark upon him; and the court of heaven decreed that "whosoever slayeth Cain, vengeance shall be taken on him seven-fold." (Gen. iv:15.) When Enoch, losing sight of all else besides, walked with Him for three hundred years, God took him away from the trials of this sin-cursed earth (Gen. v:27.), and when Noah was found righteous before God, notwithstanding, it repented Him that he had made man and in wrath and indignation he had decided to destroy him in a universal overflow, he directed this, the only holy man in all the world, how he might save himself and his family from the Deluge.

CHAPTER XII.

Having spoken at length of the many opportunities afforded Methuselah, let us now see if any evidence can be brought to show that he utilized them or not; for, unless evidence can be produced to show that he was in disfavor with God, then we must confess that he died and was sent out of the world to escape some approaching danger, and is happy with the blest. In order, therefore, that we may have a clear knowledge of the case before us, I shall first attempt to prove to you that he was rejected of the Lord, and, secondly, that his death was one of soul, as well as body.

First. As to his being rejected, we observe that it is the nature of God to always select the worthy ones to carry out his great plans. For instance, Moses was sent from leading the sheep of Jethro to lead the Israelites, though Joshua and Caleb were both in Egypt. The Levites were chosen priests, though Simeon and Judah were both older as tribes. The sons of Jesse looked

kingly, but the Lord touched not the prophet until
the ruddy youth David came in; then he said to
Samuel, "Arise and anoint him; for this is he."
(1 Sam. xv:12.)   Esau was Isaac's first born
son, and justly loved by him as heir to the throne
of opulence and birthright of power, but he was
not a fit man to be father of so great a people
as from whom a Savior should be born, and circumstances gave Jacob the birthright and the
blessing.   David was anxious to build a house for
the Lord, but the Lord waited until he was dead
and let his son Solomon build it, saying (1 Chron.
xxii:10), "He shall build a house for my name;
and he shall be my son, and I will be his father;
and I will establish the throne of his kingdom
over Israel forever."   Yea, and when we, of our
own volition, had become apostates to the prince
of darkness, aliens from God, fit subjects for eternal condemnation, our Lord, listening to the penitential prayers of fallen man, determined to inaugurate a plan to rescue him from his helpless
state.

Through Adam all had died, and, in order to
open a way for man's admittance into the kingdom
of God, justice demanded that some one should
die to satisfy his claims; hence the search to find
some one who was worthy to die for the sins of

the world. Many, no doubt, were willing; but,
to satisfy the claims of justice, the vicarious offering must be without spot or blemish, in order
to be worthy. A strong angel (Rev. v:2-9) was
given the Book of Redemption, and he cried with
a loud voice, "Who is worthy to open the book
and to loose the seal thereof?" If, then, none
but the worthy are accepted with God, it follows
that whosoever is rejected of God is unworthy.

Methuselah was, as has been shown, in a position to tower head and shoulders above every
other man who lived in his day. At the time
when God pronounced an end to all flesh, from
point of advantages, he was more able than any
man on earth to undertake the stupendous task
of saving representatives of all the animal kingdom; but hear the decision of the Judge of heaven
and earth: "The end of all flesh is come before
me; for the earth is filled with violence through
them; and, behold, I will destroy them with
the earth." (Gen. vi:13.) From this we are
able to form some idea of the universality of mortal wickedness at that time; and we would be
justified to decide that there was not a single,
solitary soul upon the earth who was worthy of
the friendly consideration of the Lord, were it
not for the exceptions made in his own words,

which I now read: "Noah (Gen. vi:9) was a just man and perfect in his generation, and Noah walked with God." And "Noah (verse 8) found grace in the eyes of the Lord." And the Lord (14) said to Noah, "Make thee an ark of gopher wood; rooms shalt thou make in the ark, and shalt pitch it within and without with pitch." "And, behold, (17) I, even I, do bring a flood of waters upon the earth, to destroy all flesh, wherein is the breath of life, from under heaven; and everything that is in the earth shall die." "But with thee (18,19) will I establish my covenant; and thou shalt come into the ark, thou, and thy sons, and thy wife, and thy sons' wives with thee. And of every living thing of all flesh, two of every sort shall thou bring into the ark, to keep them alive with thee; they shall be male and female."

This, therefore, excuses Noah and his sons, and his wife and his sons' wives from being counted *particeps criminis* in the wickedness of that time; and that we may know that he was active in the spiritual as well as the physical salvation of the world, Peter holds him up before us, names the surrounding circumstances, that no one might doubt which Noah he speaks of, and calls him a "preacher of righteousness." (2 Peter ii:5.) But, in searching the Scriptures from Genesis to

Revelation, we have been unable to find a single suggestion or reference that we could use as evidence that Methuselah was interested in the salvation of men, or concerned about a hope of heaven.

CHAPTER XIII.

METHUSELAH LOST.

The Bible is a very explicit book, and every thought expressed in it is given by inspiration of God (2 Tim. iii:16), and is made so plain (Hab. ii:2) "that he may run that readeth it." Noah (Gen. vii:6) was six hundred years old before the flood came; and, lest some should err, and say the flood came at some time during the sixth century of Noah's life, the sacred historian has surrounded the fact with a breastwork of explanations and references that remove all shadow of doubt as to the exact time of the flood.

The sixth verse of the seventh chapter of Genesis says, "Noah was six hundred years old when the flood of waters was upon the earth." The eleventh verse of the same chapter reads, "In the sixth hundredth year of Noah's life, in the second month, the seventeenth day of the month, the same day were all the fountains of the great deep broken up, and the windows of heaven were opened." The twenty-eighth and twenty-ninth verses of the ninth chapter of Genesis read thus: "And

(52)

Noah lived after the flood three hundred and fifty years." And, lest some future higher critic should say he was only approximating dates, the writer of the book of Genesis, sums up the life of Noah before and after the flood, and says (in the same verse), "And all the days of Noah were nine hundred and fifty years."

Praise the Lord for the explicitness of His Holy Word. So clear, so definite, that "the wayfaring men, though fools, shall not err therein." (Isa. xxxv:8.)

If, as we have shown by a comparison of the dates given in the fifth chapter of Genesis, Noah was born in the year ten hundred and fifty-six, and was six hundred years old when the flood came, then it follows that the date of the flood was the year sixteen hundred and fifty-six. But, as we have shown, Methuselah died in the year sixteen hundred and fifty-six; then Methuselah died the same year in which the flood came. But the waters began to fall on the seventh day of the second month of that year; then it is conclusive that Methuselah died between the first day of the first month and the seventeenth day of the second month—or less than forty-seven days before the flood of waters began to fall.

But the doom of the world was sealed one hundred and twenty years before the flood, and twenty years before the sons of Noah were born. (Gen. vi:3.) And since, as we have shown, Methuselah died the same year in which the flood came, it was sealed one hundred and twenty years before the death of Methuselah. No one need doubt or be misled about the wickedness of the world at the time when God chose Noah to build the ark. At that time (1536) Adam had been dead six hundred and six years; Seth, four hundred and ninety-six years; Enos, three hundred and ninety-five years; Cainan, three hundred and one years; Mahalaleel, two hundred and forty-six years; Jared, one hundred and fourteen years; and Enoch, who, walking with God, ascended into heaven fifty-seven years after the death of Adam, had been gone from the sin-cursed earth five hundred and forty-nine years. Lamech was six hundred and sixty-two years old, and Noah was a youth of four hundred and eighty summers, neither married nor burdened with children.

The doom of the world was sealed, and everything must perish in the universal ruin, except whom God had found worthy and perfect before him. And that no one might think he referred to the entire family when he said "Noah, have I found righteous," He named the persons who were to be saved with him. Yes, thank God, their names are all given; and nowhere between the lids of the Bible can we find evidence to prove that any other person was included. And we, as teachers of God's word, have no right to exonerate any person who lived at that time from the crime of "being corrupt before God," except those eight persons whose names are given.

But one hundred and twenty years before the flood, all the world except Noah and his three sons, and his wife and his sons' wives, was corrupt before God, and doomed to die. And since, as we have shown, Methuselah died the same year in which the flood came, then the logical conclusion is that when the doom of the world was sealed Methuselah was also corrupt before God and doomed to die. But God says (Ezek. xviii:4), "The soul that sinneth it shall die," and (Ezek. xxxviii:9), "If he do not turn from his way, he shall die in his iniquity;" "For the Lord (Neb. i:3) will not at all acquit the wicked." From this it is evident that the doom sealed upon Methuselah was effective upon his soul, as well as upon his body; for the Psalmist tells us that "the wicked shall be turned into hell with all the nations that forget God," (Psa., ix:17), and that we may know something of the torture of hell, the

Savior gives us two pictures, one in the parable
of the "wedding garment," where (Matt., xxii:
13) he says, "There shall be weeping and gnashing of teeth;" and the other in the parable of
Dives and Lazarus, where he represents the rich
man after death in the following sad words:
(Luke, xvi:23-24) "And in hell he lifted up his
eyes, being in torment, and seeth Abraham afar
off, and Lazarus in his bosom; and he cried and
said, 'Father Abraham, have mercy on me, and
send Lazarus that he may dip the tip of his finger in water and cool my tongue; for I am tor-
mented in these flames.' "

As Methuselah traveled along life's highway
from the cradle to the grave, conscience would often plead with him, no doubt, and urge him to
turn away from the evils of the world and follow
in the footsteps of his father, Enoch, who walked
with God until he left the world.

The funeral knell of various ones passing away
from time to eternity would, no doubt, ring for
a season in his ear like distant peals of thunder
that give warning of a storm, and urge him to
"prepare to meet his God." The sweet influence
of the Holy Spirit, striving to win him over from
the crooked way of sin and folly, often exerted
its beneficence upon him as it led Enoch away

from the carnal lusts of the flesh into the kingdom of God. And, though none of these things moved him to repent, the mercy of God allowed him to live on.

Onward the centuries pass, leaving Methuselah at the close of each, further and further away from God; further and further from the light of heaven. I can see him walking along life's highway. His face has been furrowed by the plowshare of centuries; his locks have been whitened with the paint-brush of Time, and hang in disheveled curls around his drooping head, like moss around the mistletoe of a leaning oak near the banks of Bayou La Teche. The finger of infirmity has touched his thigh, and his step is no longer quick and agile, but slow and cautious. His sight is dim and he has lost his way. Amid the fog and smoke of sin that surround him on every hand, he travels on, he knows not where. As the huntsman, lost in the woods, is apt to wander further away from the open path as he tries to find his way out from among the entanglement of shrub and underbrush, so Methuselah goes deeper and further into the darkness of sin as the memory of past events fades from his mind; still, the mercy of God allowed him to live on.

Wickedness continues to grow, and God has de-

clared an end to all flesh. The time of fulfill-
ment has been set for one hundred and twenty
years hence. Methuselah hears the King of Glory
talking with Noah about the wickedness of the
world and His determination to destroy the same.
He hears the Lord God reading the specifications
of the ark to Noah, and instructing him how to
erect the same. According to the directions given
in the sixth chapter of Genesis, the ark was five
hundred and fifty-five feet long, ninety-two feet
wide and fifty-five feet high. Noah was ordered
to build it three stories high. He could have had
on the first two stories of this wonderful ship
one thousand rooms ten feet square and eighteen
feet from the floor to the ceiling for the various
animals, a suit of twelve rooms of like dimensions
for himself and his family; and still had the entire third floor containing 910,800 cubic feet of
space as a storeroom for his food supplies. Methuselah sees his grandson and great-grandsons
preparing to undertake this stupendous task, without even so much as advising or suggesting a single thing worthy of notice, and still the mercy of
God allowed him to live on.

He watches them daily as they work away trying to build the ark according to the command of
God. He hears the people deriding them, and is

sufficiently able to warn them of their folly, but he takes no part, asks no questions, offers no assistance, gives no ear to their preaching, advises no one to believe them, benefits no one by his long life and varied experience; and still the mercy of God allowed him to live on.

The ark is completed, and he sees Noah and his sons gathering grain supplies to board the animal kingdom of the world for one year. He sees representatives of all the life-breathing animals gathering around and entering the ark, as if cognizant of what would happen. He sees Noah and his sons, and his wife and his sons' wives, preparing to embark upon a voyage that shall not end until the entire world except those in the ark shall have been destroyed; and, having reached the nine hundred and sixty-ninth milestone in the journey of his life, Methuselah fell lifeless in the arms of death, and the Scriptures say he died.

But what profit was all his long life to him?. What noble deed had he done? What effort had he put forth to check the onrushing tide of the sin and immorality of his day? What influence had he exerted for good? What precept or example had he set for the uplift of man or the glory of God? Not one. You cannot say, dear reader, that history was fragmentary, and the good deeds

of many who lived before the flood were not recorded. I tell you, my friends, everything that
was done before the flood to greatly influence the
civilization of that day was recorded, and told to
future generations. Even the names of the most
important children, with date of birth and length
of life, were all made a matter of historic record.
(Genesis v.) It is hardly reasonable to suppose that the same historian who so carefully
recorded in detail all the *minutiae* concerning the
antediluvian patriarchs would fail to tell of the
achievements of him who enjoyed the greatest
longevity, if he had done a single thing worthy of
historic note. He lived nine hundred and sixty-
nine years, and all that the sacred historian could
say of him was, "He died." Died! What a statement to come from the lips of God! Died in rela-
tion and influence upon future generations! Died
to the heart, and mind, and thought, and lips of
all the world! Died, and his name does not appear
again in all the Bible, except the two places,
where, for chronological exactness, it could not
be avoided. (1 Chron. i:3, and St. Luke iii:27.)
Died, to rise no more until at the last day, when
all shall appear before the judgment seat of
Christ. Well said are the words of Caesar,
"Sometimes the immortal gods allow those whom

they wish to punish for their crimes a longer exemption from punishment, and at times even better prosperity in business, in order that they may feel their punishment the more when it comes, by reason of a change of circumstances." Thus it seems to have been with Methuselah. After living through nine hundred and sixty-nine years, he escaped the Deluge by his death, only to awake in the lake that burneth with fire and brimstone. Is it to be wondered at that such a man, on the morning of the resurrection, will cry for the rocks and mountains to fall upon him and hide him from the face of an angry God? I tell you, dear readers, his conscience would bear witness against him; and, though angels should plead the merits of a Savior's blood, Methuselah would be forced to exclaim:

"Show pity, Lord; O, Lord, forgive;
And let a dying rebel live;
Yet, if my soul is sent to hell,
I must confess, Thou judgest well."

CHAPTER XIV.

REASONS FOR INVESTIGATING THE LIFE OF METHU-
SELAH.

Many who read these pages will, no doubt, won-
der why I should spend so much time and thought
to prove that a man was lost whom all the writers
of all the past have called one of the "holy fa-
thers," and regarding his long life as only an illustration of the possibility of human existence,
have been satisfied to. let slumber unnoticed and
unknown. But when it is remembered that there
is nothing in all the Bible which is not there for
a specific purpose, and to teach some great truth,
then we can see the worth of the admonition of
the Apostle who said (Acts xvii:11), "Search the
Scriptures daily, whether those things were so."
Again, "All Scripture is given by inspiration of
God, and is profitable for doctrine, for reproof,
for correction, for instruction in righteousness:
that the man of God may be perfect, thoroughly
furnished;" and many of the so-called "worthless
passages," which the casual reader and biased
(62)

student would pass unnoticed, are pregnant with far more real depth of meaning than many of the passages upon which they write pages of comment. If God is omniscient and omnipotent, then we must accept it as an axiom that He had knowledge to see the end of the world from the beginning of time, and power to control the thoughts and pen of the sacred writers, that they could not utter a word other than that which would serve to further the ends of His great plans; and I believe the day will come when all the higher critics, and the worldly wise men who have done so much to pick flaws in the various passages of Scripture, whose depth of meaning they cannot fathom, will bow in humble submission to the mandates of God, and accept His Word, whether they can comprehend it or not, as their only guide-book to life eternal.

Another reason for investigating the life of Methuselah is the fact that the God whom I serve as the Captain of my salvation is a just God; and if I, by investigation, could find a single one whom He, holding up as an example, had taken into the kingdom of glory without making any reference to him as being interested in works of righteousness or the salvation of men, then I would, from that day forward, erase from my Bible that passage of the Scriptures which tells me to bring under subjection every carnal desire; for surely the Lord will not send me to hell for doing the same things that others did who are happy with the blessed. But, in searching the Scriptures, from Genesis to Revelation, I fail to find any difference in the dealings of God toward the sons of men. Job said, "If I sin (Job x:14), then thou markest me, and thou wilt not acquit me from mine iniquity." David said (Psa. li:3), "My sin is ever before me." Solomon said (Prov. xiii:21), "Evil pursueth sinners." The Preacher said (Eccl. xii:14), "God shall bring every work into judgment, with every secret thing, whether it be good, or whether it be evil." Paul said, "Be not deceived; God is not mocked: for whatsoever a man soweth, that shall he also reap." (Gal. vi:7.) And Peter, who was with Christ, the Author of our hope, during his entire ministry, gives the following evidence (2 Peter ii:4-9), "If God spared not the angels that sinned, but cast them down to hell, and delivered them into chains of darkness, to be reserved unto judgment; and spared not the old world, but saved Noah the eighth person, a preacher of righteousness, bringing in the flood upon the world of the ungodly; and turning the cities of Sodom and Gomorrah into ashes condemned them

with an overflow, making them an ensample unto
those that after should live ungodly; and delivered just Lot, vexed with the filthy conversation of
the wicked: the Lord knoweth how to deliver the
godly out of temptation, and to reserve the un-
just unto the day of judgment to be punished."
Not satisfied with these, I pertinently ask the King
of Glory for a statement upon the subject, and in
answer He thunders from the hills of Zion through
the prophet Ezekiel, saying (Ezek. xviii:4), "The
soul that sinneth it shall die." I study the lives
of the Bible heroes, and I find that the end of all
those who strayed away from God and did not
return is shrouded in mystery and uncertainty.
This forces me to smite my breast with my hand
and say to my sin-stained soul:

> I must be careful how I live,
> Lord, give me righteous fear
> For I must give account to Thee.
> For all my actions here.

CHAPTER XV.

Do not, for a moment, dear reader, think that I have launched upon a sea of speculation in dealing with a subject hitherto unnoticed. I have not allowed myself to use other than the Word of God as proof of the correctness of my position upon the subject. I am not unmindful of the fact that my argument is at variance with all former teachings concerning Methuselah, but I feel easy in my conscience, because I have written what, in my mind, seems to be the truth concerning him; and praying the Holy Spirit for guidance, I have jotted down my thoughts as they have come to me, from time to time, and tried to arrange them in such a way that all who read them will be led to search the Scriptures.

I like the invitation given from God, through Isaiah, who wrote (Isa. i:18), "Come now, and let us reason together;" and I hail with delight the mandate of heaven delivered by Peter, when he said (1 Peter iii:15), "Sanctify the Lord God in your hearts: and be ready always to give an answer to every man that asketh you a reason of the hope that is in you." The Preacher said (Eccl. vii:25), "I applied mine heart to know and to search, and to seek out wisdom, and the reason of things, and to know the wickedness of folly, even of foolishness and madness." Isaiah said (Isa. xli:21-22), "Produce your cause, saith the Lord; bring forth your strong reasons, saith the King of Jacob. Let them bring them forth, and shew us what shall happen: let them shew the former things, what they be, that we may consider them, and know the latter end of them."

You cannot say that these passages of Scripture refer to a certain people or to a certain period of the world's history; for Jesus said, on one occasion (Matt. v:17-18), "Think not that I am come to destroy the law, or the prophets: I am not come to destroy, but to fulfil. For verily I say unto you, till heaven and earth pass, one jot or one tittle shall in no wise pass from the law, till all be fulfilled." The substance of the law is this (2 Cor. v:10), "We must all appear before the judgment seat of Christ; that every one may receive the things done in his body, according to that he hath done, whether it be good or bad." And that no one may think it optional with them as to their appearance at the final judgment, the judge of the supreme court of Israel has handed down a decision from which there can be no appeal. He says (Eccl. xii:13-14), "Fear God, and keep his commandments: for this is the whole duty of man. For God shall bring every work into judgment, with every secret thing, whether it be good, or whether it be evil."

Since, then, all must appear before the judgment seat of Christ, whether we would or would not, it behooves us, as aspirants to life eternal, to study the life and character of every Bible hero, that we may know whether, from the facts given in the Scriptures, that life is in accord with the life of Christ, and be able to give a reason for the hope that is in us.

There is an inexplicable intuition that causes the human heart to know those who, by birth, are its relatives; so also, the child of God should study to know who are his relatives: first, by the witness of the Spirit (1 John v:10); and, secondly, by the kind of fruit they bear (Luke xiii: 9). For "by their fruits (Matt. vii:20) ye shall know them."

This is in keeping with the teachings of the Bible, which declare, and prove by numerous illustrations, that the way of holiness is an highway (Isa. xxxv:3), straight (Jer. xxxi:9) and narrow (Matt. vii:14); and few there be that find it. But we, after speculative theorizing to make the sacred word of God harmonize with our earthly wisdom, seek to point out a way whereby all of the patriarchs of the Bible died in the full triumph of faith, and went sweeping through the pearly gates into the city of God. This gives hypocrites an opportunity to hope on through their wrongdoings. There are those who will lie, steal, cheat, break the commandments, and grieve the Holy Spirit in a thousand ways, and, pointing with injured innocence to some hero of the Bible who did the same things, they fold their arms in undisturbed peace and rejoice to tell you that they are on their steady march to heaven and its immortal glory.

CHAPTER XVI.

FACTS WORTH KNOWING.

Some tell us that the long life of Methuselah was of great worth to the world in passing knowledge from Adam to Noah without the intervention of another generation, whereby some of the facts might not have been known. They say the fact that he was with Adam during two hundred and forty-three years of his life, and with Noah for six hundred years causes the life of Methuselah to overlap the lives of Adam and Noah in such a way that there can be no possible chance for a mistake in the information given from one to the other. And, again, they say the life of Methuselah is of vast importance, because it is a link in the very essential chain of chronology from Adam to Christ.

They forget the fact that the chronology of Christ's earthly ancestry was no more perfect than that of any mortal, and is given only as a matter of history that we may trace his lineage back to the father of the human race, and first

(70)

transgressor of heaven's law. As to the importance they attach to the life of Methuselah for passing knowledge from Adam to Noah, I am surprised that men of great learning should even discuss it. From the death of Adam to the birth of Noah spans a bridge of only one hundred and twenty-six years, across which walked Enos, Cainan, Mahalaleel, Jared, and Lamech. Enos was contemporary with Adam for six hundred and ninety-five years and with Noah for eighty-four years. Cainan was with Adam six hundred and five years, and with Noah one hundred and seventy-nine years. Mahalaleel was with Adam five hundred and thirty-five years, and with Noah two hundred and thirty-four years. Jared was with Adam four hundred and seventy years, and with Noah three hundred and sixty-six years. And Lamech was with Adam fifty-six years, and with Noah, as his father, five hundred and ninety-five years.

From this it is clearly evident that the life of Methuselah is not an absolute necessity for historic record from Adam to Noah. It serves only to show the wonderful opportunity given him to have interlaced his life and name like a thread of gold into the warp and woof of all that happened before the flood. But, alas for him, like many

of those who live to-day, he just lived, and that
was all.   Disinterested, unconcerned, he lived;
and all that could be said as a funeral sermon was
"He died."

The sun sets behind the western hills, but the
trail of light which it leaves athwart the sky
guides many a pilgrim to his distant home.   The
trees of the forest wither and die, but in the lapse
of ages they are dug up as coal to keep the sons
of men cheerful and warm amid the chilly blasts
of winter.   The coral insects die, but the reefs
they raise break the surge on the shore of a con-
tinent, or form an island in the bosom of the ocean
as a home for some shipwrecked mariner.   But
Methuselah lived nine   hundred   and   sixty-nine
years and died, and has never been heard of since.
Not even the Son of God, who was mindful of
the sparrow and the ant and the lily, is recorded
as having so much as even mentioned his name.
He was dead, and the sum total of his life's worth
was told when the sacred historian said, "He
died."

The text, then, serves to teach us that it is not
the length of a life, but the influence it has exerted upon those with whom it has come in contact, that determines its worth in the economic
needs of the world.   Methuselah lived nine hun-

dred and sixty-nine years, and his entire life history, with all of its achievements, is told in a single sentence: "And all the days of Methuselah were nine hundred and sixty-nine years, and he died." On the other hand, Jesus Christ lived only about thirty-three years, and with all the writers of all the world telling of his achievements, not half has ever been told of the wondrous works of the Son of God. From the cradle to the grave, Christ was ever looking for, and grasping, opportunities to lift mankind to a higher civilization, and make the world better for his having lived in it; while Methuselah, with a life of nine hundred and sixty-nine years, is not accredited by any writer of prose or poetry, fact or fiction, as having done, or even attempted to do, a single thing in the world but live and die.

Not a single writer of the Scriptures makes any reference to him or mentions his name, except where for chronological exactness, it could not be avoided. (Luke and Chronicles.) Longevity was the theme of every sacred writer, and yet, not one of them mentioned Methuselah, though he enjoyed it to a greater extent than any other mortal that ever lived. He had opportunities which were given to no other man, but he allowed them all to pass, and to all time to come he was dead. And so also to-day there are men and women who, living amid opportunities of every kind for bettering the stock of the human race, are doing nothing for themselves, nothing for the uplift of mankind, nothing for the glory of God. They are just living, and when life is over, all that can be said of them is that they lived and died.

CHAPTER XVII.

A Page in Alabama History.

Think of the commanding position in the affairs of this nation Booker T. Washington, a former slave, has attained by grasping the opportunities as they have come to him from time to time.

At the meeting of the last Alabama Legislature it was the thought of many politicians that the Tuskegee Normal and Industrial Institute, of which he is the President, and from which no revenue of tax was collectable, was a menace to the county in which it is located. Attention was called to the fact that the institution owns more than two thousand acres of the county's land, for which no tax was paid. It was shown by logical reasoning that the rapid growth of the school would soon bankrupt the county by monopolizing the land from which the county might obtain a revenue of tax if it were not for the laws which prevent the taxing of school property. The State ordered that an investigation be made and

(75)

reported, so that the Legislature might adopt measures to relieve the county of its embarrassment.

The investigation was made by Mr. W. W. Haralson, Public Accountant. He reported that he had examined the books and accounts of the institution as directed, and made diligent inquiry into every department of the same. He gave a brief history of the rise of the institution from the rented shanty in which it began in 1881, with thirty pupils and one teacher, up to its mammoth proportions of to-day. He told of the various departments of learning connected with the institution; of the facilities for training boys and girls for honorable and industrious citizenship; of the exactness with which every detail of finance connected with the school is kept, and declared that, looking at its purely business side, "The school is the model of perfection."

He told of the experiments with cotton, whereby the institution is trying to improve the quality of Alabama's crops by crossing the various grades of cotton in the hope of increasing the length of the staple. He said he was favorably impressed with the condition and care of the grounds, the excellent order prevailing everywhere among the students, and the general air of earnestness and

industry that seemed to pervade the entire estab-
lishment.

He said the institution owned two thousand
four hundred acres of land, which it had bought
from the county at an expense of $14,057.50,
after the land had been returned to the county
for delinquent taxes. His report showed that
twenty-nine pieces of property owned by persons
directly connected with the school had increased
in tax valuation, by the growth of the school, from
$4,320 to $27,786 for the present year. And thir-
ty-eight other pieces of property owned by persons not at all connected with the school had increased in tax valuation, by proximity to this
great and growing institution, from $1,050 to the
amount of $16,244. He then called attention to
the fact that the school has an endowment fund
of $1,479,150.81; has an average attendance of
1,500 pupils; employs 149 teachers; collects un-
paid legacies, through the banks of the county,
over $633,000 each year; spends $125,000 in the
county each year; and, besides all this, owns min-
eral lands in the Northern part of the State to
the amount of 25,000 acres, the value of which
would exceed $200,000.

The investigation showed that the Tuskegee
Normal and Industrial Institute was not a cancer,

gradually sapping the financial life out of the county, but rather the spinal cord from which the county receives its nerve energy of tax valuation and business and commercial activity. The subject of taxing school property not only died of its own weight, but I am told by one whose veracity is not doubted that many of the legislators were heard expressing regret that Booker T. Washington and his wonderful institution were not located in their county.

Now, tell me, dear reader, do you believe such a man could escape the notice of future writers of this day and generation? No, my friend, the men and women who have greatly aided in the advancements of civilization and the uplift of mankind are never forgotten upon the pages of history, for they are the nucleus from which the history grows. Dorcas made garments and distributed them to the poor, and the facts were told by the sacred writers. One woman gave the last penny she had in a church collection, and it was recorded. Even the woman who, rejoicing because Christ had rid her of devils, hid under the table and kissed the feet of the blessed Redeemer until her tears of joy falling upon them made them so wet they were wiped away with the locks of her hair, will awake in the morning of the

resurrection and find that her name is recorded
in the Word of God. But Methuselah, lived nine
hundred and sixty-nine years and did nothing,
either good or bad, whereby his name might be
mentioned after saying, "He died." When I think
of the idlers and the loafers, and the indifferent
men and women about us, and consider the opportunities which they have for improving their
own condition, and the condition of those about
them, I am reminded of the man whose only earthly possession was a large diamond that was worth
many thousands of dollars. On the deck of an
ocean steamer one day, while going from America,
he amused himself by tossing his diamond up and
catching it as it fell. Flushed with pride at the
attention he attracted, he tossed his diamond higher and higher, until, overcome with pride at the
applause of the crowd, he tossed his diamond up
with all his might, and, to his dismay and un-
doing, missed it; saw it bound over the side of
the ship, strike the water and sink into the sea.
The one legacy that is bequeathed to every man is
"an opportunity;" and, oh, the numbers who, like
the"fool with a fortune," are tossing their diamond
opportunities away in lustful pleasure and carnal gratification; and when they are dead, all that
can be said of them is that they lived and died.

CHAPTER XVIII.

METHUSELAH A WARNING TO SINNERS.

Methuselah is a warning to sinners. They see signs of a coming flood, and know that "We must all appear before the judgment seat of Christ;" yet they reject all offers of mercy and pardon, and seem utterly indifferent with reference to their soul's eternal welfare. They know that all opportunities for heaven will be shut off when they leave these mundane shores, and the uncertainty of life makes it impossible for human knowledge to even approximate the hour of death, and yet they seem as unconcerned as though the story of the cross were a mythical joke.

Our Savior, anxious to save men from the thraldom of sin, even when he, of his own volition, had become an apostate to the prince of darkness, laid aside his royal paraphernalia, disrobed himself of all the happiness that heaven offered, came down to this sin-cursed earth, incarnated himself in a fading robe of feeble mortality, became subject to all the ills and afflictions to which the flesh is heir, and, as a preacher of righteousness, became so very poor he was forced to perform a miracle to pay his tax as a citizen. (Matt. xvii: 27.) No home, and but a few friends, he at one time exclaimed: "The foxes have holes, and the birds of the air have nests; but the Son of man hath not where to lay his head." (Luke ix:58.)

Betrayed into the hands of his enemies by one of his bosom friends, he was dragged about the streets of the city in chains, blindfolded, scourged, spit upon and maltreated until almost ready to faint from exhaustion, hunger and thirst. A crown of thorns was pressed down upon his head, causing the blood to gush from his temples and dye his garments red. They led him out from the city, forcing him to bear his own cross. Weak from loss of blood and nerve exhaustion, Christ stumbled and fell, but the heartless murderers, shorn of every vestige of mercy, scourged him until, staggering, he regained his feet and proceeded forth "as a lamb to the slaughter." Christ could have delivered himself, or had legions of angels at his command; but he suffered himself to be crucified and die upon the shameful cross that he might satisfy the claims of justice, and appease the justly-kindled wrath and indignation of an insulted Creator.

He was buried in a tomb, but arose again on the third day, thereby proving his identity as the Son of God. He spent forty days upon earth after his resurrection, instructing his disciples how to build up his church, which, like the ark of Noah, is to save all who serve him of every nation, tribe and tongue, from the coming conflagration when this old world of ours shall burn as an oven. Having finished his work on earth, Christ ascended into heaven and took his seat at the right hand of the Father, where he is still pleading for you and for me. Even now he stands with outstretched arms, saying to every sinful soul, "To-day, if you hear my voice, harden not your heart; but come unto me, and I will give you rest."

Christ's plans for building the church, like God's plans for the ark, are very peculiar, and full of mystery to the unregenerated mind. He himself said (Matt. x:16), "Behold, I send you forth as sheep in the midst of wolves." "Fear not them which kill the body, but are not able to kill the soul: but rather fear him who is able to destroy both soul and body in hell." (Matt. x:28.) "Behold, the devil will cast some of you into prison, that ye may be tried; and ye shall have tribulation: be thou faithful unto death, and I will give thee a crown of life." (Rev. ii:10.)

The followers of Christ show their desire to obtain the crown by doing all they can to build up the church, and help hasten the day "when the kingdoms of this world shall become the kingdoms of our Lord and of his Christ." Like Noah, they preach righteousness and warn you of the coming flood. You, like Methuselah, stand outside, and give no ear to their entreaties to you to come in ere it is too late.

Reason teaches you that he who spoke worlds into existence, and formed out of nothing the universe with all its myriads of systems, must be infinitely happy and glorious in himself. He is omniscient in wisdom, and His power is bounded only by eternity. His felicity and dignity can neither be enlarged nor diminished, and think for a moment how great must be the condescension, and how infinite the love and mercy of God must be that he should ask for reconciliation with a poor, wretched rebel and traitor, whom He might blot out of existence by the breath of His nostril. Hear Him who created worlds, and caused myriads of creatures to live and move by the fiat of his awful word, calling in tender tones and pleading with a poor, ignorant, wayward, dependent sinner, to "Come now, and let us reason together;" saying in tones of pity, "Though your sins be as scarlet, they shall be as white as snow; though they be red like crimson, they shall be as wool." No matter how blackened your soul may be; no matter how foul the deeds of your past life; no matter how far you are alienated from God and the light of heaven, you may come, and are especially invited to come and be saved upon the terms of the gospel; and yet many go on heedless of God's offered mercy, like the poor, starving, homeless wanderer who refused to accept alms or lodging, and died without food or shelter.

When Alexander the Great encamped before a city, he used to set up a light, and all who would come to him while that light lasted, would be kindly received and given quarter; if not, then, after the light had gone out, no one need expect quarter or mercy. God sets up light after light, and waits year after year, and still his offers of mercy are rejected. You get a glimpse of the warning light from time to time, as those who are near and dear to you are swept off from the shores of time by the waves of death into the ocean of eternity; and you know from the aches and pains that haunt your life that it is but a short time when you must follow. Ever since Adam heard the voice of God in Eden telling him

"Thou shalt surely die," man has been vainly seeking some way of escape from the grim monster, Death. Whether he make his home in a gilded palace, the drapery and fine linen of which challenge for a comparison the apostle's vision of heaven; or whether he dwell in a tent in the lonely woods, where nothing save the hooting of the owls disturbs the lonesome silence of his solitary abode, man finds himself ever and anon face to face with the grim monster, Death, who follows him as a cat would a mouse, to devour him as an insufficient morsel for his hungry stomach. In vain have philosophers and scientists sought to free the inhabitants of earth from this dread monster, whose gluttonous appetite devours all that earth produces, and is still unsatisfied. Kingdoms and nations, dynasties and empires have been erected, and labelled "Imperishable," but the powerful claws of this merciless beast have broken them to pieces, and he has devoured them with relish. Constantly feasting, he is always famished; eating without intermission, yet starving and poor. He ravishes the world of every object, animate or inanimate, without reference or concern as to age, size or shape, and yet this hoary-headed hydra is lean and bony as though he had starved for a hundred years. All efforts to shun him are as vain foolishness, and you know not how soon the summons will come, "Thy soul is required of thee." (Luke xii:20.) Like one who sees his boat drifting down the Niagara River towards the falls, but fails to pull ashore, you seem utterly indifferent, though drifting further and further away from the moorings of Christ, and nearing the terrible, deafening, death-dashing rapids of a moral, or spiritual, or an eternal cataract. Will you not heed the voice of God, and, grasping the oars of faith, pull for the shore of a hope in Christ Jesus before it is too late?

O, that I had the voice of a trumpet, that I might disturb the auditory nerve of your spiritual ear and arouse you from the stupor into which you have fallen. Like a swift-sailing vessel without helm or rudder, you are tossed hither and thither by the mad winds and waves of thoughtless impulses. You imagine yourself rich, great and powerful, healthy and happy, when, in reality, you are deceiving your own soul, and your incoherent babbling gives a lie to all you have to say concerning your wealth and influence, "For every beast of the forest is mine, and the cattle upon a thousand hills" (Psa. 1:10), and "the silver is mine, and the gold is mine, saith the Lord of Hosts." (Hag. ii:8.) In chains, you sing of freedom, and while utterly helpless, you are anxious to help reform the church and assist the true-born children of God, whom you imagine are in a state of need.

You remind me very much of a man whom I saw the other day while passing the guard-house. The officers of the law were trying to take from the patrol wagon an insane man, whom they had picked up. He was dirt, ignorance and depravity personified; and yet, to the amusement of a large crowd, he was gesticulating wildly with his hands, and declaring that he was a god, and the officers would all die if they dared to touch his holy body. With feet and hands securely bound, and utterly powerless in the hands of the officers, he was writhing and calling for all those who needed assistance to call upon him, and receive a blessing. As he was being borne into the guard-house to be locked up in a cell, he shouted, "Hear me, ye mortals, don't come too close, for if any of you touch my holy body, you will immediately drop dead."

CHAPTER XIX.

No Excuse for Rejecting Christ.

Are you delaying because you think there is time enough? It has well been said, "Procrastination is the thief of time." The proud Queen Elizabeth rejected the offers of mercy, and on her death-bed exclaimed in the agony of her soul, "My kingdom for a moment of time." In the life of Steven Grellet we are told that once, when Miss Roscoe was in the room of Tom Paine, some of his infidel associates came to him, and, in a loud, heartless manner, said, "Tom Paine, it is said you are turning Christian, but we hope you will die as you have lived," and then went away. Turning to Miss Roscoe, Paine said: "You see what miserable comforters they are." Once he asked her if she had read any of his writings; she told him she had begun "The Age of Reason," but it made her so miserable that she flung it in the fire. "I wish all had done as you did," he said, "for, if the devil ever had any agency in any work, he had it in my writing that book." When going to carry him refreshments, she repeatedly heard him uttering the language, "O, Lord! Lord God!" or "Lord Jesus, have mercy on me."

In the midst of life we are in death, and, since our life is so uncertain, and all opportunities for correcting mistakes are taken from us when we leave the walks of life, it is very necessary, my sinner friend, that you accept God now, and make him your friend, that

> "When thy summons comes to join
> The innumerable caravan which moves
> To that mysterious realm where each shall take
> His chamber in the silent halls of death,
> Thou go not, like the quarry-slave at night,
> Scourged to his dungeon; but, sustained and soothed
> By an unfaltering trust, approach thy grave
> Like one who wraps the drapery of his couch
> About him, and lies down to pleasant dreams."

Are you laboring under an hallucination that you can escape the all-seeing eye of God? Lafayette, the great friend of George Washington, tells us that he was once shut up in a small room in a gloomy prison for a long time. In the door of his cell there was a very small hole. At that hole a soldier was placed day and night to watch him. All he could see was the soldier's eye; but that eye was always there. Day and night, every moment when he looked up, he always saw that eye. There was no escape, no hiding, when he lay down, and when he rose up, that eye was watching him. And so it is with the eye of God. It is in every cloud on the mountain; in the secret chambers of every muttering thunder; observes every wind that bends the forest, and sees every ray of light that falls from the sun. Where can you go from his all-seeing eye? And where can you hide and escape His presence? David said (Psa. cxxxix:8-10), "If I ascend up into heaven, thou art there: if I make my bed in hell, behold, thou art there. If I take the wings of the morning, and dwell in the uttermost parts of the sea; even there shall thy hand lead me, and thy right hand shall hold me." At every step, and in every circumstance, there is the eye of God. Even in the central darkness of your innermost soul the eye of God watches and knows the thoughts of your heart. "His going forth is from the ends of the heaven, and His circuit unto the ends of it" (Psa. xix:6), and he says to the children of men (Rev. iii:8), "I know thy works."

Are you delaying because you doubt the existence of a true and living God? "The devils (Jas. ii:19) believed and trembled." The heathen believe, and, having lost the identity of the true God, worship wood and stone, in the belief that they have found that ideal for which their spirits thirst. Did you ever notice the works of a watch?

There are large wheels and small wheels all fitted together so as to concur in an orderly motion. Did you ever for a moment think that the watch came together by chance? Did you ever go through a magnificent building and believe it happened there by chance? Can you think of a palace beset with pleasant gardens, adorned with stately avenues, furnished with well-contrived aqueducts and cascades, and equipped with everything for convenience, and then persuade yourself to believe it is all a matter of chance? How, then, can you contemplate the world in which you live, furnished with air, light, gravity, heat and everything that is necessary for its preservation and security; fitted with everything conducive to the life, health, happiness, propagation and increase of all the prodigious variety of creatures with which the earth is stocked; with nothing wanting, nothing redundant or frivolous, nothing botching or ill-made, but everything, even in the appendages, exactly answering all its ends and occasions; and then doubt the existence of a Being sufficiently wise to intelligently plan and execute the wondrous work?

The quince tree may have its true limbs torn away, and the limbs of other trees grafted in their stead until twelve manner of fruit may ripen thereupon, but the body of that tree will ever retain its identity; and every shoot that sprouts upward from the roots will, upon examination, prove to be unadulterated quince trees. So also with man. He is a worshipful being, and, though he may have grafted into his mind thoughts and teachings that tend to allure him away from God, and give ease from the fear of death, by filling his mouth with argument, and his thoughts with delusive hope; yet, away down at the root of his heart's innermost soul, there is a consciousness of the existence of a Supreme Being, and,

> "A thousand stings within his breast,
> Deprive his soul of ease."

CHAPTER XX.

God's Leniency With Men.

Methuselah shows us how patient and merciful God is, even with those who oppose His will. Henry Ward Beecher said, "The thought of the future punishment for the wicked which the Bible reveals is enough to make an earthquake of terror in every man's soul. I do not accept the doctrine of eternal punishment because I delight in it. I would cast in doubts, if I could, till I had filled hell up to the brim; I would destroy all faith in it; but that would do me no good. I could not destroy the thing. Nor does it help me to take the word everlasting and put it into a rack like an inquisitor, until I make it shriek out some other name. I cannot alter the stern facts."

Methuselah was the son of Enoch, and the grandfather of Noah: both men of such extraordinary piety that they are described as walking with God; and, though he, as an individual, does not appear connected with any of the movements of his day for the uplift of mankind, he was allowed to live on.

Noah was a righteous man, and walked with God, and, notwithstanding Methuselah's moral and spiritual lethargy, it would have been an appalling sight for Noah, while securely housed in the ark, to have seen his grandfather tossing on the surging waves of the swelling flood. And thus, for all we know, God, of respect for Noah's righteousness, and to remove from him any temptation to open the ark or endanger the safety of those within, stayed the liquid mountains and the water-filled clouds until the old man Methuselah was dead, and his grandson had buried him with the other antediluvian patriarchs.

And so it is to-day. Many of those who are enemies of Christ are blessed, and their lives prolonged from day to day, through the prayers and righteousness of some relative or friend who is walking with God. Mercy is shown to them for the sake of Christ, who pleads their cause before the throne of God. If, however, that sinner is not influenced to turn to God and live, and go on heedless of the mercies shown, heedless of the long life given, heedless of the many opportunities offered, though he should be spared until the frosts of an hundred winters have fallen upon him, yet, at the last day, the mercy of Christ will be turned to wrath, and, when begging to be re-

leased from the clutches of the evil one, Christ
will turn away and laugh at his calamity, and
mock when his fear cometh. Instead of running
to his rescue, He will say to the prince of darkness, "Bind him hand and foot, and take him
away, and cast him into outer darkness; there
shall be weeping and gnashing of teeth." (Matt.
xxii:13.)

God demands our belief in His great and sol-
emn warnings. He calls us to fear. He has revealed to us the way. His son is the ark, the
door is open, and he urges every one to enter and
be saved upon the terms of the gospel. Upon this
your safety depends. "For there is none other
name under heaven given among men, whereby
we must be saved." (Acts iv:12.) Will you believe and enter, or will you, like Methuselah, spend
your life amid opportunities for heaven, and die
without a hope in Christ Jesus the Lord? Though
the flood was delayed for one hundred and twenty
years, it surely came, and so will your end come;
though now you appear able to withstand the
trials of years unnumbered.

CHAPTER XXI.

THE PRICE OF THE ARK.

As I have previously said, the ark of Noah was a boat of wondrous size, and as ship-building was then in its infancy, it is not to be wondered at that Noah and his sons were one hundred and twenty years completing it. To build the ark, according to the plans and specifications given Noah, required at least five hundred thousand feet of beams, sills and scantlings for the framework; one hundred and eleven thousand feet of lumber for the side; nineteen thousand nine hundred and sixty-five feet for the ends; four hundred and four thousand eight hundred feet for the top, bottom and second and third-story floors, and eighty-nine thousand feet to divide the first and second stories into twelve hundred rooms each eighteen feet from floor to ceiling, and ten feet square, with a partition ten feet high, to prevent the wild beasts of the forest from preying upon each other and thwarting the divine plan for the preservation of the various species. Thus Noah and his sons, of necessity, were compelled to procure and dress

(96)

not less than one million, one hundred and twenty-four thousand seven hundred and sixty-five square feet of lumber for the building of that wonderful ark, which was to save representatives of all the life-breathing animals. The lumber alone required for Noah's ark, if purchased to-day at a minimum price of $20 per thousand, would cost $22,495,300, besides the labor, nails, bolts and pitch necessary to make the ark waterproof, and able to ride the waves of a shoreless sea for one year. All this expense and time and labor and thought were given to save representatives of God's creation.

And so also with the ark of Christ. Each person in the Godhead wrought in the work of building an ark for the saving of man from the coming conflagration when this old world shall burn as an oven. "God so loved the world, that he gave His only begotten Son, that whosoever believeth in Him should not perish, but have everlasting life." (John iii:16.) Christ died an ignominious death upon a shameful cross as a legal transgressor, that he might satisfy the claims of justice and redeem man from the curse of a broken law. (Gal. ii:16.) And the Holy Ghost, leaving the kingdom of glory, has been wandering around the earth ever since the day of Pentecost, seeking timber for the ark of Christ, by establishing the

kingdom of God in the hearts of men. He, like
Noah, is ever preaching to you through the voice
of conscience. He stands at the door of your
heart even now, and, however much you try to
break away from His beneficent influence, you
are constantly reminded of the fact that you must
appear before the judgment seat of Christ.
Christ's kingdom, like the ark of Noah, is suffi-
cient to save representatives of every kindred,
tribe and tongue.

In the twenty-first chapter of Revelations we
are told that heaven was measured with a golden
reed, and found to be twelve thousand furlongs in
length and breadth and heighth. Twelve thousand furlongs are equal to seven millions, nine
hundred and twenty thousand feet; and since the
length and breadth and heighth of the city are the
same, we find by cubing the length, that heaven
is a four square city containing nine hundred and
forty-eight sextillion, nine hundred and eighty-
eight quintillion cubic feet. Let us reserve one-
half of this vast domain for the throne of God and
the choir of heaven and the hundred and forty
and four thousand white robed elders of the courts
of glory. Then let us reserve one-half of the re-
maining half for streets and avenues; and the re-
maining one-fourth part of heaven will be sufficiently large to be divided into five trillion, seven

hundred and forty-three billion, seven hundred and fifty-nine million rooms, each of which would be nineteen feet square, and sixteen feet from floor to ceiling. Now let us suppose that the world always did and always will contain nine hundred millions of inhabitants. And let us suppose that the world will stand for a hundred thousand years to come. This would give an aggregate of twenty-seven trillion persons. Now let us suppose that in the universe there were eleven thousand, two hundred and thirty other worlds equal to ours in population and length of duration, and that all the people from all those worlds through all those years were righteous and destined to spend eternity with God: even then, there would be a room nineteen feet square, and sixteen feet from floor to ceiling for every one of them, and yet there would be room for millions more.

He says to you, while reading this book, "Come unto me, all ye that labor and are heavy-laden, and I will give you rest." (Matt. xi:28.) His Holy Spirit, even now, is knocking at the door of your heart, and asking you to let Him come in and "teach you all things, and bring all things to your remembrance, whatsoever Christ has said unto you." (John, xiv:

26.) This gives every one an opportunity to come to Christ and be saved. He says (Isa., lv:7) "Let the wicked forsake his way, and the unrighteous man his thoughts: and let him return unto the Lord, and He will have mercy upon him; and to our God, for He will abundantly pardon." Why not arouse thyself, O, thou modern Methuselah, and turn away from the thraldom of sin, and find rest in the ark Christ Jesus.

Unless from your sins you return and repent,
To hell, like Methuselah, you will be sent.
Oh, turn, sinner, turn, and to Jesus now fly,
And plead for forgiveness. Oh why will you die?
The joys of earth pleasures and hopes are all vain;
And naught, in the end, can they promise but pain,
Like spectres of horror they'll glare in your eye,
Oh, turn, while the Saviour asks, "Why will you die?"

CHAPTER XXII.

METHUSELAH A WARNING TO CHRISTIANS.

There are many people who boast of the long time they have been a member of the church, and' "Remember the day and hour when God, for Christ's sake, spoke peace to their soul." They forget that past blessings will not suffice, and that the getting into the kingdom of God is a result of "working out the soul's salvation."

Methuselah was a member of the church of his day—a righteous family—and with pride could boast of the fact that he had been a member of it for centuries; but what profit was it to him if, as an individual, he did nothing to help it in the work of saving the world from the curse of sin? He lived in it, and that was all; for nowhere do we find his name associated with any movement of any kind. Nine hundred and sixty-nine years he was a member of the church concerning which the poets sing, and yet not one even so much as mentions his name. All the sacred writers of the Bible shunned his name as though it were a loathsome disease. No illustration, no comparison, no reference is made to him or his longevity by any of the writers from Genesis to Revelation. The Son of God was mindful of every sparrow that falleth to the ground (Matt. x:29-30), and notes the number of hairs in every human head. He used the grass of the field, the flower of the garden, the various animals, insects, reptiles, mountains, stones and every phenomenon of nature to make plain his way of salvation; and yet he is not recorded as even so much as calling Methuselah's name. He was dead from the lips of all the world, and dead to all glory yet to come. And so it will be with many of those whose names have been on the church record for years. They are too busy to attend any of the services; too intelligent to endure the ignorance of the worshipers of Christ; too morally pure to become contaminated by associating with sinners saved by grace; too cultured to drink the sacrament of the Lord unless some physician can vouch for the perfect health of all those who have tasted before the cup is offered them; too busily engaged with worldly pleasures to bow in prayer; too fearful of the reproach of society to seek and to save those who are lost; too full of self for the kingdom of Christ.

When Napoleon I. invaded Egypt he encountered an army that defied all his military genius.

They were entrenched within a mud fort. If the fort had been built of rock, he could have blown it up with powder, or shivered it with his artillery; if it had been made of wood, he could have fired it with rockets; but it was nothing but a huge mass of mud into which his iron missiles stuck fast, and only increased its force of resistance. So it is with many of those who belong to the church. They are fortified within a mud fort of church membership, and no missiles from the preacher's gospel gun can reach them, because they belong to the church. They take no part in the services, attend worship only when the occasion is a rare one; they seek to make no heart glad but their own; they soothe no brow; no one in distress do they comfort. Their whole life is spent for their own happiness, and, having done nothing, there is no need to mention their names after the funeral service is over.

CHAPTER XXIII.

THE TRIUMPH OF CHRIST.

The Christian religion is full of glory to God and good will to men. Unlike the religion of the heathen, which deifies wood and stone; or the religion of those who appease the anger of their deity by acts of violence, the Christian religion is heavenly in its origin; heavenly in its actions; heavenly in its tendency. Like the water which is raised from the ocean by the magnetic waterspout, and borne on the wings of the wind to distant parts of the earth, escapes from the custody of the clouds, descends upon the earth in the form of rain, blesses the world with its cool, refreshing powers, but refuses all offers to stay, and will not stop to slumber until, through channels, it has reached its native ocean; so the Christian religion, emanating from Christ, rests not in the bosom of those who possess it, until with them, it is safe in the ocean of Christ's eternal love. Thus the man or woman who has the Christian religion finds himself drawn closer and closer to

Christ, until, overshadowed by the transcendant beauty of his personality, he shouts with the Apostle, "I know that my Redeemer liveth, because He lives in my soul the hope of eternal glory."

The Christian religion makes its possessor a blessing to every sphere in which he moves, for its whole character is summed up in the love of God and the love of man. That is all; and the sorrowing and the suffering that the Christians bear cause rejoicing in the heart, because of the great love that possesses them and pales into insignificance any affliction borne for the object of their affections. It was this that caused Noah and his sons to work away at the ark amid the jeering criticisms and unbelief of a doomed world. It caused Daniel to count death in a den of lions nothing, and the three Hebrew children to scorn the heat of a blazing furnace. It has inspired thousands of its possessors to walk cheerfully into the throes of a violent death, and caused Christ, the Christ of every man or woman who will be saved, to allow himself to be crucified at the hand of a merciless mob, that man, whom He loved, might be saved.

It has translated the Bible into every known tongue, and pressed civilization into the lands beyond. It has changed the babbling songs of the heathen into notes of praise, and transformed the wigwams into houses and palaces, around the sacred altar of which truth loves to dwell. Great buildings for scientific research it has built over the decayed ruins of superstition and falsehood; and the church—the home of wisdom—it has placed on every hillside, valley and plain.

Mark Anthony drove two lions hitched to his chariot through the streets of Rome; Jesus spoke, and the winds and the waves were guided by the power of his word. Alexander stood on the shore of the Mediterranean Sea when he had drenched the world in blood, and wept because there were no more worlds for him to conquer; the Son of God wept over a lost and ruined world, and shed his own precious blood that we might have a right to the tree of life. Achilles chased Hector around the walls of Troy three times, and slew him with his sword; the Son of God chased Death three days through the voiceless silence of the dreamless tomb, and, forcing him into open combat, foiled his power, wrenched from him his sting, bound him to his chariot wheel, and liberated us from the throes of that terrible enemy. Xerxes led a million well dressed soldiers to battle; Jesus Christ led a hundred and forty and four thousand elders, and an innumerable white-robed throng from the domain of sin into the kingdom of God. When Titus overthrew Jerusalem and laid waste the land of Cainan, the Romans honored his achievements by the erection of a triumphal arch to commemorate his conquest. The obelisks of Egypt remind us of the reign of the ancient Pharaohs, and a sarcophagus of Egyptian marble was used by the French to emphasize their appreciation of the achievements of their illustrious Napoleon. In every city and town, monuments and statues are erected in honor of the illustrious sons of earth, whose conquest and victory were in their lifetime, nor lasted longer than a few years after their decease. The conquest of Jesus, on the other hand, was endless in duration, and his victory is from everlasting to everlasting. His triumph still goes on, and is fast approaching that fullness when "the kingdoms of this world shall become the kingdoms of our Lord and of His Christ."

When cities shall have passed away, and we are able only in imagination to walk their crowded streets and admire their grandeur; when civilization, like a weary traveler along a dusty road, shall confess it can go no further, and lie down to rest neath the shade of the millenial dawn; when the kingdoms of this world shall have been decomposed into the smelting caldron of omnipotence, and moulded into one great kingdom for Christ; yea, when human achievements shall have crumbled neath the iron-clad hoofs of Time, and Time itself, with all its possibilities, shall have been sunk in the shoreless sea of eternity; even then, as we sit by the crystal stream, along the banks of which millions of the redeemed host are chanting their song, if we listen we can hear in ever-rippling wave and rustling leaf praises to Him whose triumph has just begun.

As in the days of Methuselah, the religious sons of God have married the worldly daughters of Ambition and Public Opinion; and of them have begat children called Honor, Fame, Wealth, Titles, Degrees, Worldliness and a host of others, who stalk through the land with giant strength, and gainsay the faithful few, who, like Noah, are toiling daily to build up the Church of Christ. Are you like the sons of Noah helping to raise the weighty timber of the Word of God? Are you cutting timber for the ark from the forests of sin? Are you helping in the completion of the ark for the salvation of man? The Church of Christ, like the ark of Noah, is built without rudder, prow or sail; and, when launched, will take no course, trade at no shore, make no trip, but just float over the waters of eternity forever and forever.

You say you belong to the church, but are you sure that you are one of those who shall have passage in the ark? You laudate the nobility of earth, and keep festive days to commemorate the birth and death of those who marshaled hosts on the battle-fields, and caused thousands of precious lives to be lost, that they might achieve a victory; where is your monument erected in honor of the leader of God's host? He never lost a battle; conquered all the combined forces and allies of death, hell and the grave.

You shout the praises of the political parasites of your party, whose only aim is to feast upon the appetizing morsel of an office fee. Have you canvassed your district for Him who liberated the great republic of this world from its debt, paying the price thereof with His own blood?

You say you have been converted, and that Christ is sovereign. Where is the emblem of His power? What statue have you raised in honor of His noble deeds. How many have you, personally, influenced to serve him? That a flood is coming, you know, both from your guidebook and from scientific research. How many have you tried to influence to enter the ark Christ Jesus and be saved? Like Methuselah, you have a great deal of time, and opportunities without number.

What are you doing with them? You say you are on your way to glory, while those with whom you walk, confess and their works prove, that they have no hope in Christ. "How can two walk together except they be agreed?" (Amos iii:3.) Can you walk and talk and live the life of a sinner, and yet be a joint heir with the spotless Lamb of God who knows no sin, and in whose mouth no guile is found? It has been well said, "Show me your associates, and I will tell you who you are; tell me the company you keep, and I will write your history."

If then, you have Christ, put on the hope of eternal glory; if you have been washed in His precious blood, and made a joint heir with Him in His Father's kingdom; if you, like Noah, would enter the ark of his glory when the world shall be on fire, then you must remember that it is your abounding duty to preach Christ and Him crucified, to every one with whom you come in contact. For, while we do not know the day nor the hour of the conflagration, yet we know it will surely come; and, though we cannot prove it as a logical syllogism, our faith gathered from the truthfulness of all else that Christ has said makes us declare this as a fact also.

The book of all human possibilities will then

be closed; the Son of God will then resign His office as mediator between God and man. Mercy will intercede for man no longer. The heat of the sun will have been exhausted; and, being able no longer to influence the solar system with its light and heat, the forces of gravity will be lost; equilibrium of the entire universe will be destroyed, and excitement will reign supreme. Amid the mighty tumult of convulsed worlds, a company of angels will fly through the heavens. Four of them will light on the four corners of the earth. (Rev. vii:1) and hold the winds that they may not blow. Another, lighting on the earth, will offer a sacrifice of incense, the smoke from which, mingling with the prayers of the saints, will reach up to heaven as a sweet-smelling odor for the King of Kings. Another shall sound his trumpet, and cause hail of fire, mingled with blood, to fall upon the earth. Another shall sound his trumpet, and every volcano shall belch forth a stream of fire and tumble into the sea. Another shall sound his trumpet, and a blazing meteor shall strike the earth, and cause the waters to taste like wormwood. Another shall sound his trumpet, and a third part of the sun, moon and stars shall be destroyed. Another shall sound his trumpet, and a star shall fall against the earth with such tremendous force a flame shall burst upon the earth from the bottomless pit, teeming with locusts and scorpions of wondrous size. Another shall sound his trumpet, and the four imprisoned angels shall be loosed to wreak vengeance upon the already distressed inhabitants of terra firmá. Another will be flying through the heavens crying, "Woe! Woe!" to the lost sinners; while a strong angel, clothed with the cloud, and a rainbow crown, will place his right foot upon the ocean and the left foot upon the land, and swear by Him that liveth that time shall be no more. Then, away above the din and wails of the lost host, will be heard the triumphant strains from countless millions of the redeemed, who, rising from their graves, shall go in with the unexpired Christians who have not tasted death, and, mingling the sweet symphonies of their thousand-stringed harps with the melody of their voices, they will rend the heavenly atmosphere with jubilation and praises of a new-made song of redemption's story; and all those who have done nothing to bring themselves into favor with Christ will be left to await for the sounding of the last trumpet, and their names shall be called "Methuselah," which is to say, "They died and were sent out from the presence of God and of the Lamb."

CONCLUSION.

I have written what, in my mind, seems to be the meaning of the word "Methuselah," and the lesson it teaches both to saints and sinners. I have not allowed myself to use other than the Word of God as a proof of the position which I have taken, and I hope you have read this book with your Bible in hand. I have tried to write in such a way that all who read these pages will be led to search the Scriptures. If I have done nothing more than this, I am abundantly paid for my pains, for I believe every traveler to the bar of God, while on earth, must be an active Christian, or a Methuselah to die and be sent out from the presence of God into the outer darkness prepared for the devil and his angels. And, although to be a member of a righteous family is an advantage, yet it will not profit us anything unless there is intrinsic merit in our own works.

The children of men, like an army of soldiers,
  Who, leaving their homes, have gone forth to the fray,
Are rushing along on the field of life's battle,
  Not knowing when death all their earth hopes shall slay.
'Twas Adam who brought death, and millions have fought
    death
  With science and art, whom as friends they did call;
But all of earth's treasures from death can't relieve them,
  For Death is a monster, and he conquers all.
But he who on Jesus' breast is reposing,
  And faithfully trying to keep God's command,
Shall triumph, though death in this life battle slay him,
  And gain as a victor's palm heaven's fair land.

Let us then, my brother, like Enoch and Noah,
  Live only for Jesus while earth's way we trod;
That all who may see us, and all who may hear us,
  Will know by our life's work, we're walking with God
Then, shouting and singing, we'll fight in life's battle,
  And scorn the proud boasting of death and the grave,
We'll rush to life's battle, and when death shall strike us,
  We'll shout home to Jesus, who's mighty to save.

Ingram Content Group UK Ltd.
Milton Keynes UK
UKHW021828030423
419563UK00007B/967